Positively Penguins!

By Kathryn Stevens

The
Child's
World®
www.childsworld.com

Published in the United States of America by The Child's World®
1980 Lookout Drive • Mankato, MN 56003-1705
800-599-READ • www.childsworld.com

ACKNOWLEDGMENTS

The Child's World®: Mary Berendes, Publishing Director

Produced by Shoreline Publishing Group LLC
President / Editorial Director: James Buckley, Jr.
Designer: Tom Carling, carlingdesign.com
Cover Art: Slimfilms
Assistant Editor: Jim Gigliotti

Photo Credits:
Cover: Main: Dreamstime.com; Insets: iStock (top),
Vaida Petreikiene/Dreamstime.com.
Interior: AP/Wide World: 28; Corbis: 12, 21 top, 25; Dreamstime.
com (photographers listed): 4, 8, David Bate 9, George Kubatyan 16,
Carolyn Morrison 15, Vaida Petreikiene 6, Arnie Rose 7, Vladimir
Seliverstov 19, 21 bottom; iStock: 10, 11, 13, 22, 27 bottom; Minden
Pictures (photographers listed): Konrad Wothe 12, Fred Bavendam
23, Tuida Roy 26, 29, Flip Nicklin 18, 23, 26, 27 top, 29.

LIBRARY OF CONGRESS CATALOG-IN-PUBLICATION DATA

Stevens, Kathryn, 1954–
  Positively penguins! / by Kathryn Stevens.
     p. cm. — (Reading rocks!)
  Includes bibliographical references and index.
  ISBN 978-1-60253-102-4 (library bound : alk. paper)
  1. Penguins—Juvenile literature. I. Title. II. Series.

  QL696.S473S726 2008
  598.47--dc22
                                2008004484

CONTENTS

ALL ABOUT
Penguins

Start with a cute, tubby shape. Add a pair of short legs and a waddling walk. Now add a beak and some stubby wings. Throw in some tuxedo colors, too! What have you got? A bird that looks like nothing else on Earth!

Many people—and tons of kids— say penguins are their favorite birds. Kids keep fuzzy, stuffed penguins in their bedrooms.

Movies and cartoons show penguins doing all kinds of amazing things. You've probably guessed that they don't really tap dance! They don't surf. They don't tunnel out of zoos. And they don't tell jokes. But they're still amazing creatures!

Penguins are the only birds that can swim but cannot fly. They look very awkward on land, waddling when they walk. But in the water, penguins are awesome! Their tubby bodies shoot through the water like torpedoes. Most birds have light, hollow bones so they can fly. Penguins have heavy bones, so they can dive underwater. Plus, their webbed feet are like swim fins. Their wings act as flippers.

Rockhopper penguins get their name from how they walk.

Penguins or Porpoises?

Penguins swim fastest when they're under the surface. But they must come to the surface to breathe. Some kinds of penguins have a way of doing both! They leap in and out of the water as they swim. This way of moving is called "porpoising." That's because porpoises and dolphins do it, too.

On land, penguins walk by taking short steps or hops. They walk slowly—maybe 2 miles (3 km) per hour. That is slower than most people walk! If they are upset, they can run faster. But some penguins have a quicker way of moving. They throw themselves down on their bellies and "toboggan" quickly across the ice!

Emperor penguins are easy to spot, with their orange bills and yellow neck feathers.

Where do penguins live, anyway? They live in the Southern Hemisphere—that's the southern half of the world. Some of them live in Antarctica, one of the coldest places on Earth. Others live on islands and coastlines of the cool southern oceans. You can find them in South America, Australia, New Zealand, and Africa. Some

live in places that are quite warm.
Galápagos penguins live on the
Galápagos Islands near the equator.

Different penguin **species** are
different sizes. The biggest are
emperor penguins. They can be
51 inches (130 cm) tall and weigh
84 pounds (38 kg)! The smallest are
little blue penguins. They're
16 inches (41 cm) tall and
weigh only 2 pounds (1 kg).

Emperor and king penguins
have patches of orange
feathers on their heads.
Other species have long,
feathery crests or plumes.
Some have unusual bill
and eye colors.

This scientific word means a group of animals that are very similar and mate only with each other.

Galápagos penguins live on islands off the coast of Ecuador.

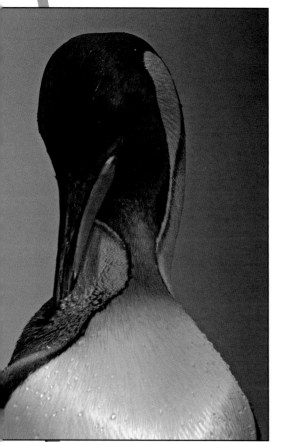

Using the sharp end of its bill, this emperor penguin makes sure its feathers are ready for swimming.

Penguins' feathers are made for spending lots of time in the water. They fit together tightly to keep out water and wind. Air trapped under the feathers helps keep the penguins warm. Penguins take good care of their feathers. They **preen** them often. They run their bills over a body part that produces waxy oil. Then they run their bills over their feathers to clean and oil them.

Once a year, the birds **molt** their old, worn-out feathers. During the molt, penguins' feathers aren't waterproof and can't keep them warm. The penguins stay out of the

water until their new feathers are in place. Since they feed only in the water, this means they go hungry! They build up extra fat beforehand to live off during their molt.

It's hard to stay warm in the cold ocean! In addition to feathers, penguins have body fat to keep them warm. On land, their feathers and fat can hold in too much body heat. To cool off, they stick out their wings and ruffle their feathers.

Time for lunch. Penguins dive under the water to track down and catch fish.

Some penguins spend up to three-quarters of their lives at sea. Some stay in the water for months! In the ocean, penguins' black-and-white coloring helps protect them. From below, the birds' white bellies blend in with the sunlight. From above, their dark heads and backs blend in with the water.

OPPOSITE PAGE
A blackfooted penguin gives you a good look at the black-and-white coloring of penguins.

For all their cute looks, penguins are deadly ocean **predators**. They eat mostly fish, squid, and tiny shrimplike animals called krill. Backward-pointing spines in their mouths help them gulp down slippery **prey**. Most of their prey live fairly close to the surface. The penguins don't have to dive down very far to catch them. Emperor penguins dive the deepest and longest, chasing after squids and fishes. The deepest emperor dive ever recorded was 1,755 feet (535 m). The longest dive by an emperor lasted 21 minutes. That's a long time to hold your breath!

2

PENGUIN Families

Penguins like to hang around with other penguins. Many species swim and hunt in groups. And many have their young in huge nesting sites called **rookeries**. Big rookeries might have hundreds of thousands of birds. Penguins usually return to the same rookeries every year.

Most penguin nests aren't very fancy. Some are just groups or rings of rocks. Some are little hills of grass or other plants. African penguins nest in burrows or under rocks or bushes. There, the eggs are protected from predators and the hot sun. Little blue penguins nest in protected spots or burrows, too. Galápagos penguins nest in burrows, or in holes or caves in old lava flows. Humboldt penguins often dig their burrows in deep layers of penguin *guano*, which is another word for poop!

This gentoo penguin chick (right) is begging its parent for some food.

This male emperor penguin checks on the egg tucked safely between his feet.

At some busy rookeries, adults compete for good nesting spots. Adélie penguins compete fiercely for safe nesting spots in the middle of the colony. They compete for stones for the nests, too. Gentoo penguins also compete for nesting materials. They gather stones, grass, or sticks—sometimes by taking them from other penguins!

Penguins often lay two eggs. In many species, the parents take turns keeping the eggs warm. One parent warms and guards the eggs. The other one goes to feed in the ocean, sometimes for days at time. Then they trade places. The eggs usually take at least a month to hatch. Then the penguin chicks chip their way through the shell.

After the chicks hatch, the parents often take turns feeding them. The parents eat food and then bring it back up to feed the chicks. The parents feed only their own babies. When there are two chicks in a nest, one of the chicks tends to be larger. It gets more of the food the parents bring.

Feed me! This gray-feathered chick gets a gooey meal directly from its mother's mouth.

Most young penguins have fuzzy, gray feathers.

Newly hatched penguins have soft, fluffy feathers. Soon they grow woollier feathers. In some species, older chicks gather in nursery groups called crèches (KRESH-ez) while their parents hunt for food. Being in a group keeps the chicks warmer and safer. Finally, the chicks grow their shiny black-and-white adult feathers. As soon as their own waterproof feathers have grown in, they can swim in the ocean. Then they can start catching their own food.

Emperor penguins do things very differently. They lay their eggs and raise their chicks in the Antarctic winter, when it's dark and unbelievably cold. They don't even build nests. Instead, they use their bodies to keep their young warm.

Female emperors lay a single egg, then go off to sea to feed. In the fierce wind and cold, the males huddle together for warmth, balancing the eggs on their feet for nine long weeks. The males don't eat during this time. In fact, they can lose a third or more of their body weight! The female finally comes back when the egg is ready to hatch. She takes the male's place while he heads to the ocean to eat.

In the Antarctic winter, temperatures can fall to -76 degrees F (-60 degrees C). Winds howl— sometimes at 125 miles (201 km) an hour! Yet male emperors are able to keep their eggs warm.

PROTECTING Penguins

3

Penguins have always faced many dangers. They can't fly, and they can't run very well. Land predators can catch them easily. That's why penguins have always lived in areas without many land predators. But people have brought predators to some of these areas, such as foxes, rats, and ferrets. These animals can do terrible damage to penguin colonies.

Many penguin-eating predators live in the ocean. Sharks, leopard seals, fur seals, sea lions, and killer whales all love to eat penguins.

And sometimes danger comes from above! Birds such as skuas, sheathbills, gulls, and giant petrels eat penguin eggs and chicks. Some of them are very clever. Skuas work in pairs. One skua attracts the penguin parent's attention, and the other steals the egg or chick.

This skua is stealing a penguin egg.

Leopard seals are fast and can chase down penguins in the water.

21

Many penguins around South America depend on cold ocean **currents** that bring food. When those currents move or change, food becomes scarce. During these El Niño (el NEEN-yoh) times, penguin populations can drop way down.

Penguins are usually not afraid of people, and visitors can often get closer than is safe for the birds.

But the greatest danger to penguins has been people. Long ago, native peoples hunted some types of

penguins and ate their eggs. But they did not kill many of the animals. The birds had no reason to be afraid of people. When explorers, whalers, and fishing boats came to those areas, penguins were an easy source of meat and eggs.

These penguin eggs were probably broken by a bird before they could hatch.

As numbers of people grew, people came to penguin areas more often. They began collecting eggs. They hunted penguins for their body fat. They turned the fat into oil for fuel and lighting. Penguin feathers were used on people's hats and clothing, and to stuff mattresses. Penguin skins were turned into purses, slippers, and hats.

People no longer hunt penguins as they did before. But they still pose a danger to penguins. Many nesting areas have been destroyed or damaged by people. Even if the nesting areas are still there, the penguins can't nest properly with too many people around. Planes flying overhead or visitors coming too close can cause big problems.

Oil spills are a danger, too. Feathers coated with **crude oil** aren't waterproof and can't keep the birds warm. The penguins can easily die of cold. And if the penguins preen, the oil poisons them. Trash thrown in the ocean can also be a problem. Penguins and other birds can get caught in

garbage or eat plastic. Large-scale fishing causes other problems for penguins. In some areas, people take too many of the fish and squid that penguins need for food. And penguins sometimes get caught in fishing nets and lines.

An oil spill on an Antarctic beach has coated this penguin with oil—and probably doomed it.

Room for one more? Shrinking ice sheets in the southern oceans are leaving less sea ice for penguins.

Global warming is a big concern, too. Rising air and water temperatures can affect penguins that live on sea ice. They can also affect krill and fish that penguins eat. Antarctica's Adélie penguins eat lots of krill. The krill need tiny plants called algae that grow on sea ice. Emperor penguins nest on the sea ice. Rising temperatures mean less sea ice. And that means less food for Adélies and less nesting area for emperors.

Today, Galápagos, erect-crested, and yellow-eyed penguins are **endangered**. That means they're in danger of dying out. Other penguin species are in trouble, too.

Krill are tiny sea creatures somewhat like shrimp.

Eggs and Guano

In the early 1900s, there were some 575,000 African or blackfooted penguins. By the late 1990s, there were only 178,000. Egg collectors took up to 700,000 penguin eggs a year! They also took the guano, where the penguins burrowed and nested, for **fertilizer**. The eggs in the nests were no longer safe from predators and the sun's heat. Egg collecting is no longer legal, but some people do it anyway.

Scientists get up close and personal while studying penguins so that the birds can be better protected.

Scientists and governments are looking at why penguin numbers are dropping. The U.S. Fish and Wildlife Service recently took steps to help emperor penguins and several other kinds. They put them under the protection of the Endangered Species Act. They want to look at how fast populations are dropping—and why. They will be looking at things such as fishing, predators, loss of nesting areas, and global warming.

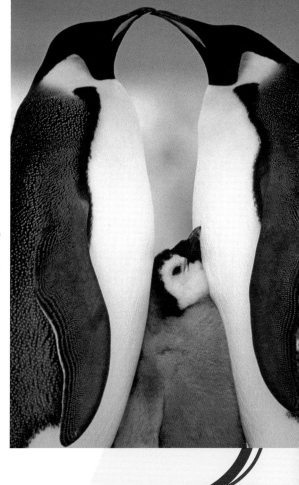

With the help of some people, this penguin chick might grow up in a safer world!

Today, laws in many countries protect all 17 penguin species from egg collecting and hunting. And many people and governments are working to keep penguin nesting places safer. Zoos and aquariums are working to raise more penguins, too. Nobody wants a world without penguins!

GLOSSARY

crude oil thick, black oil from under the ground

currents streams of water flowing within the ocean

endangered close to dying out

fertilizer material added to soil to help plants grow

molt to get rid of an old, outer layer of skin, shell, hair, or feathers

predators animals that hunt and kill other animals for food

preen in birds, to slide the beak along the feathers to clean and tidy them

prey animals that other animals hunt as food

rookeries large nesting areas used by many animals at once

species a group of animals that share the same features and can have babies only with animals in the same group

FIND OUT MORE

BOOKS

Arctic and Antarctic
by Barbara Taylor (DK Children, 2000)
If you'd like to learn more about the polar regions and the plants and animals that live there, this is the book for you.

Penguins Swim But Don't Get Wet
by Melvin Berger and Gilda Berger (Scholastic, 2004)
This fun and interesting book has tons of fascinating facts about penguins.

Poles Apart: Why Penguins and Polar Bears Will Never Be Neighbors
by Elaine Scott (Viking Juvenile, 2004)
Ever wonder why penguins live only in the Antarctic and polar bears live only in the Arctic? This book answers that question, and lots more.

WEB SITES

Visit our Web site for lots of links about penguins:
www.childsworld.com/links

Note to Parents, Teachers, and Librarians: We routinely check our Web links to make sure they're safe, active sites—so encourage your readers to check them out!

INDEX

KATHRYN STEVENS has used her love of nature and the outdoors to write many books for young readers. She has written about bugs, snakes, gorillas, grizzlies, and even fleas!